Live Well,

Love Much,

Laugh Often

Live Well,

Love Much,

Laugh Often

Anecdotes for Life

Janet Alario

© 2004 by Janet Alario. All rights reserved.
2nd Printing 2014

Trusted Books is an imprint of Deep River Books. The views expressed or implied in this work are those of the author. To learn more about Deep River Books, go online to www.DeepRiverBooks.com.

No part of this publication may be reproduced, stored in a retrieval system, or transmitted in any way by any means—electronic, mechanical, photocopy, recording, or otherwise—without the prior permission of the copyright holder, except as provided by USA copyright law.

Unless otherwise noted, all Scriptures are taken from the Holy Bible, New International Version, Copyright © 1973, 1978, 1984 by the International Bible Society. Used by permission of Zondervan Publishing House. The "NIV" and "New International Version" trademarks are registered in the United States Patent and Trademark Office by International Bible Society.

Scripture references marked KJV are taken from the King James Version of the Bible.

Scripture references marked NASB are taken from the New American Standard Bible, © 1960, 1963, 1968, 1971, 1972, 1973, 1975, 1977 by The Lockman Foundation. Used by permission.

ISBN: 978-1-63269-047-0
Library of Congress Catalog Card Number: 2004095187

For God:

Thank you for the blessing
of Your Holy Spirit
who works through
each and every one of us.
May we each find that in life
which energizes us,
discover our gifts,
and offer them back
to You and one another for Your glory.
I am eternally grateful
for my family,
their unconditional
love and support,
and for God enabling me
to become
a product of His love
and mercy!

"Janet Alario has written a book that reflects her deep love for God and her passionate desire to convey that love to others. Her transparency and vulnerability help the reader identify with the different challenges we all face as Christians. But Janet doesn't stop with the challenges. Her message of faith, hope, and love through Jesus Christ will inspire you to seek His face like never before."

> Mary Ann L. Diorio, Ph.D., CLC
> Author/Speaker/Life Coach

Table of Contents

Chapter 1: Letting Go 9
Chapter 2: Come Alive..15
Chapter 3: Being Truly Present 23
Chapter 4: A Symphony of Prayer......................29
Chapter 5: Anticipating One Another's Needs....35
Chapter 6: Clearing Away the Clutter 39
Chapter 7: Forgiveness..43
Chapter 8: Choosing Our Response 49
Chapter 9: Live Each Day As Though It
    Were Our Last 53
Chapter 10: Keep a Sense of Humor 55
Chapter 11: Loneliness..59
Chapter 12: All We Need Is Love 65
Chapter 13: Get Rid of Grudges Daily 69
Chapter 14: Trust Him 73
Chapter 15: Harmony in Nature 79
Chapter 16: Detachment 83

Chapter 17: Discerning Interruptions.................87
Chapter 18: Abandoning Our Vices.....................93
Chapter 19: Suffering Well................................101
Chapter 20: The Rewards of Hope....................109
Chapter 21: The Art of Compassion 113
Chapter 22: Hang On and Enjoy the Ride!.......119

Chapter 1

Letting Go

On a recent business trip my husband, Charlie, and I took, I clutched onto my bag as though my whole life was in it. It only contained my things. Why was I so reluctant to give it to the attendant who persistently followed me since check-in at the airport? He was trying so hard to convince me to release it to him. "It will not fit in the overhead compartment," he said repeatedly. I only became more adamant in keeping it with me.

I cried like part of me was being taken away when he handed me a tag and said: "You may retrieve your bag in Houston." Was it so bad that I would be without my boredom busters? All the distractions I needed to keep me from thinking too much were being surrendered. Or, was I upset because I would be delayed during our connection? There was ample time to retrieve it.

I began to think of the poor people on the space shuttle, Columbia, which had exploded only 15 minutes before landing earlier that week. How did they feel leaving their families, friends, and belongings behind in pursuit of their dreams? How much trust and fortitude did it take to do that?

I want to release my fears to God. I know He has a call for me and for each one of us. So why do we always want to be in control of our destiny? Why do we feel the need to control the outcome of every situation? It's truly a humbling experience when we finally realize that we can't. I want to walk in humility, but I'm not able to without God's omnipresence guiding me.

As I put my head back on the narrow, upright chair, relief finally came to me. I felt free from the load I was carrying. Forfeiting my luggage was not so bad after all. Hey, I could get used to this. I thought about my parents who were home running our household, supervising our three teenage children while we were gone. I didn't want to bother them to take over while we were away. I always had to be independent. *Never show your weakness by asking for help*, I'd fool myself into believing. To the contrary, others seek the opportunity to be as needed and useful as we do.

Of course I had to get everything done before I left because nobody could cover for me. It was my work, and I wanted to do it all—the housecleaning, cooking, driving, shopping, bookkeeping, and anything else I could do to make people need me. *Don't forget to exercise and look beautiful*, I'd remind myself. It made me feel that I had a purpose in life. Why couldn't I see that people love me simply for who I am? I know God does. Could they? I want so much to love my family for who they are and not just for what they accomplish.

Our oldest son, Anthony, is a pilot now. How can it be that a seventeen-year-old could get a pilot's license? Who were "they" that justified his knowledge and experience were substantial grounds for licensing one so young? Or was it I, refusing to believe that he could do it? I've always pictured the plane in the palm of God's hand taking us from one place to the other. Could I let my son pursue his dream and release my fears?

When I flew with Anthony in that small plane, I prayed that he might realize it was not only his skill that was involved, but also God guiding him in wisdom and understanding. One stormy day, it took a very rough landing for him to humble himself and hand over the controls to the instructor, whom I thanked for coming along in spite of Anthony's license. Anthony is an excellent pilot. His discernment is obvious. On calm days the ride was smooth and pleasant; I was the one who needed to trust God in watching over him. In the same way that Anthony had to ask for help during that storm, I must reach out to those who want to help me.

Yes, God sends many humbling experiences our way. I only pray that we take those opportunities for what they're worth and learn from them. I strive to walk in humility all the days of my life. I recall the prayer of St. Francis of Assisi:

> "Lord, make me an instrument of Your peace. Where there is hatred, let me sow love. Where there is injury, pardon; where there is doubt, faith; where there is despair, hope; where there is darkness, light; and where there is sadness, joy.
>
> "O Divine Master, grant that I may not so much seek to be consoled, as to console; to be understood, as to understand; to be loved, as to love; for it is in giving that we receive; it is in pardoning that we are pardoned; and it is in dying that we are born to eternal life."

The world has such a warped sense of values. We're so easily fooled into believing the better things in life are tangible. Relationships are what it's all about. Charlie always said: "We can't take the money with us when we die. It's our relationships that matter in this life. We cannot measure our worth by our success or monetary value. It doesn't matter where we eat; it's the company that is important." He is so right.

In order to gain something, we must make room for it in our lives. Letting go will enable us to do so. In emptying ourselves, we can find the time, energy, and interest to experience what God has in store for us.

Chapter 2

Come Alive

I was always one to change my plans to accommodate others; but, somehow, this time I knew I shouldn't. Charlie was planning yet another business venture; and he asked me to join him. I was in a dilemma. Do I change my plans, as I usually do, or should I hold fast and do what I had committed to do? I thank God for giving me the confidence to experience what was important to me and keep my plans to go to the "Come Alive" seminar I signed up for at a local Christian college.

What a revelation! The college offers such wonderful classes to nourish and educate us in God's wonderful ways. The whole weekend was a blessing. I was filled with the Holy Spirit guiding me in what He has called me to do in a better way. I began to see my glass as half full rather than half empty. What a rude awakening. To think I would have missed this wonderful experience if I had dismissed what I thought was important.

Why do we tend to look at our situations in life as discouraging and overbearing when, really, they are glorious opportunities for us to love and serve God and others better? Our attitude toward any given situation gives us a strong hold to either conquer or be destroyed by our circumstances. Knowing that God is always with us, how can we entertain the thought of being overcome with despair? I remember His promises:

> "I have told you these things so that in me you may have peace. In the world you will have trouble. But take heart! I have overcome the world."
>
> Jn 16:33

> "The Lord is good, a refuge in times of trouble. He cares for those that trust in Him."
>
> Na 1:7

We can make all the plans we want to, but it is His will that shall prevail. Of course, we must constantly be listening to His promises along the way. This will enable His Spirit to dwell within us and show us the way. We must pray for the ability to apply God's word to our lives. I had a whole new outlook on life. We could really make a difference in this world with such optimism. What a wonderful opportunity to turn a situation around and see our lives through the eyes of God.

When we're in the company of positive people, don't they make us feel better? It seems like they light up the room with their optimism. I can feel myself transform into a happier person in their company. At the same time, negative people drag us down. Their pessimism can really dampen our spirits.

We can be that radiant light to others simply by choosing to see our situations in life as blessings rather than curses. We're enabling God to use us through our suffering as a method of conditioning us to become better people. We can learn compassion, patience, discipline, and so many more virtues simply by accepting our circumstances and saying, "yes" to God. We can be the vehicle God needs to carry out His plans. Didn't Mary display that in her response to God's request of her?

> "I am the Lord's servant," Mary answered. "Be it done to me as You have said."
>
> Lk 1:38

We must refuse to be affected by negativity. I've heard Joyce Meyer say that when we walk into a room, we shouldn't be a thermometer, but a thermostat. A thermostat controls the temperature in the room; a thermometer is affected by it. We can set the mood around us by radiating a pleasant, appreciative, and warm response to all that life throws at us. Let's catch that ball and run with it. We will quickly feel the joy in doing God's work. We have a choice to grow as we age or wither and die. I want to **grow** old—not wither away like a dried up weed.

By taking a keen interest in my work, no matter how trivial the task, I realized how full of life I became. Whether I was doing laundry, scrubbing toilets, making beds, cooking, shopping, or doing paperwork, I felt alive and present in all that I was doing. I'd dedicate all my chores to God and expect no recognition from anyone in return. I'd consider my efforts a form of praise and thanksgiving for my blessings. My home was the blessing; therefore, cleaning became my way of thanking Him for it. My business was the blessing; so doing the paperwork became my praise for His gift of my work.

See how quickly the rewards flourish when we see our efforts as a form of prayer? Waiting for my family to recognize my work no longer was an issue. I don't have to feel appreciated by anyone, because I know in my heart that I'm working for God. Disappointment was no longer welcome . . . I had no room for it.

I began serving my family dinner in the dining room and using all of the good dishes and silverware. Why do we always save them for company? Since the most important people in our lives are the ones we live with, why not treat them that way? Eating becomes dining and an opportunity to hear concerns of our loved ones. We started to really listen to each other without the usual interruptions. After all, what are families and friends for but to love, talk to, care for, and listen to? Pope John Paul II referred to the family as the "domestic church."

Miraculously, what goes around comes around. Soon Charlie and our children began to have servants' hearts. They wanted to reciprocate. Linda, brought us breakfast in bed one morning. Anthony fixed things quickly, and diligently. Nancy began shopping, cooking, and cleaning her bedroom and bathroom. We preach God's word in our actions using words only when necessary.

I hope when guests visit our home, they're greeted with welcome hospitality. We learn what we live with. The power of God is so healing. Our actions can influence those around us for better or for worse. Why not choose better?

Didn't Jesus try to show us how serving others is the way we serve Him? He washed the feet of His disciples! He was constantly serving others, and He asks us to do the same. Think of the endless possibilities for hope and encouragement. How can we expect our children to react reasonably if we ourselves don't?

I was determined to make our home reflect the peace and tranquility I longed for. Lights beneath the plants paint a softness on the walls. The fish tank brings life into the room. Spiritual music sounds so inspirational. Fountains of soothing water bubble vivaciously, and the smell of fresh-baked bread fills the air with a sweet aroma. Making it in the breadmaker is so easy.

A fire glows warmly, and we surround ourselves with fresh flowers and plants. Softly-lit candles create calmness. Overstuffed bowls of fruits and nuts give you a welcome invitation. We wallpapered the rooms with pictures of fun times we've had together with friends and family.

A picture of Jesus laughing is a focal point over the fireplace. It reminds us that He is bigger than any of our problems. The natural sounds of birds chirping offers a cheerful feeling. Aesthetically, our home is an informal place for friends and family to enjoy one another's company or simply to bask in the peace of Christ.

The kids and I took classes together such as art, knitting, sewing, and cooking. We planted a garden, learned how to can fruits and vegetables, and make fresh pasta. All of these activities bring us closer together and enable us to spend time enjoying one another's company. The funny thing is that it didn't cost a lot of money. If we planned trips together, it would have been more expensive and not as memorable because we wouldn't be creating traditions.

We discovered a sense of belonging. We now find security in our home and family and feel fulfilled with the Spirit of God. We play games at night in order to relax, providing there isn't too much homework or studying to do. We listen to spiritual songs and appreciate the positive messages they offer. Our happiness becomes contagious. People around us are hooked on the uplifting words.

Chapter 3
Being Truly Present

I know I have to learn how to listen better. It's a common complaint among my children. I multitask, pretend I'm listening, and then defend myself in saying the kids don't tell me anything. It's so much easier to change our own behavior than to expect others to change. When people talk to me, I find myself thinking of the next thing I have to do or say. I want desperately to live in the moment and not worry about the future. I realized I was eccentric when I dropped my daughter off at her dance class one night. I pulled into the lot and pulled right out again, without dropping her off. Yes, life was moving too quickly for me. I had to slow down and become present in what I did.

Why are we constantly anticipating the next move? Who, what, where, when, and why are the questions that continuously torment us. Nancy told me how intently her boyfriend, Chris, listened to her. She had mentioned to him that she didn't have time to copy the last page of her book, so he did it for her and brought it into school the next day so she wouldn't have to carry the book around. Just think of how happy we would all become if each one of us did such thoughtful acts of kindness for others.

We think it is so hard to understand people. We never know what experiences they've had in their lives that cause them to be the way they are. Why not think more compassionately? It would certainly help us to calm down when driving or when irritated over trivial matters. So many misunderstandings would be eliminated.

If we listen better and give the other person the benefit of the doubt, we'd be better equipped to anticipate their needs. When we're understood, we respond more positively to one another. We can cultivate our relationships rather than watch them deteriorate right before our eyes.

It's in giving that we receive. If we give abundantly without expectations, both love and joy will manifest within our hearts. Think of a mother and her child. When my children were small, I didn't expect them to thank me for changing their diaper or feeding them. My reward was a happy, comfortable child.

It's the same with serving. I guess that is why I love to be around children. They live in the present moment. They're not worried about the next thing they have to do or how they're going to do it. I'm sure that's why God considered children precious in His sight. They trust completely and have no fear. We can certainly learn a great deal from them. They have such a zest for life and are so forgiving. Mark 10:14–16 instructs us:

> "When Jesus saw this, He was indignant. He said to them, ' Let the little children come to me, and do not hinder them, for the kingdom of God belongs to such as these. I tell you the truth, anyone who will not receive the kingdom of God like a little child will never enter it.' And He took the children in His arms, put His hands on them, and blessed them."

I've had the pleasure of teaching children about God for six years now. Every time I think I could be using the time to get more of my work accomplished, as if anything else is more important, I'm humbled and enriched by the exuberance of these children. They look directly into my eyes with their warm smiles and truly make me feel needed. They are joy in its purest form. I can feel their love embracing me simply by their questions and stories. I've learned so much from them, and I'm grateful for the opportunity to serve them.

Through helping Nancy, in the nursing home, I've learned a great deal. The residents mainly suffer from Alzheimer's disease. Now they're certainly living in the present. Again, each situation I encounter has helped me realize how much more we experience life by staying in the moment. They neither regret the past nor fear the future.

On an occasion when we were making Valentine's Day cards, one woman said to me, "We have to do this when our loved ones are alive, not after they die." I was amazed at her wisdom. She could have taught the busiest of people a lesson. I had the pleasure of speaking to another woman for about an hour. Of course when I went back the following week, she didn't remember me. It's only the here and now that she was concerned with.

At work, the chances to satisfy our customers would be infinite. I used to think of customer complaints as a nuisance. Now I consider them a timely method of expediting a solution to the problem I wouldn't have even known about had they not taken time out of their busy schedule to advise me. This also saved us a large fee for a mystery-shopper service. We simply placed a sign with an 800 number in all our stores. When a complaint would come in, first we'd say "Is it true?" If it was, we'd thank and reward the person for bringing the issue to our attention, then we'd take corrective action. What we do is not as important as how we do it, but why we do it is most important. God is referred to in Genesis as "I Am." Could He be encouraging us to remain in the present as He is?

Chapter 4
A Symphony of Prayer

Why do people say: "I've done everything I can; now all I can do is pray?" The first thing we should do is pray. Just think, when we hear an earful of problems we have no idea how to solve, rather than offering our unwelcome advice, we could say: "Let's pray about it together." This allows God to come in and help us with His omnipotence. Without prayer, it's like asking a neighbor to care for our garden without telling them we have a shed full of tools to help them do the job.

We fool ourselves into believing that we don't have time to pray. Prayer is hope, and in everything we do we are hoping to accomplish something. Whether it's to complete a job, earn a degree, help someone, develop a skill, lose weight, or just feel better. Life always involves movement, change, and unforeseen circumstances. So why are we waiting for life to become calm for us to stop and pray? We must work with what we've got to make it as satisfying as we can and pray, or hope, unceasingly as we go along.

I'm sure we all have bittersweet relationships with our computers. Well, mine was trying to converse with me in a language I didn't comprehend; and I was frustrated. I had a great deal of work to accomplish that day, and we were trying to get away for the weekend. After many attempts to solve the problem myself, I resorted to asking the kids to help me before they left for school. Of course, that was unsuccessful.

Later on, I called my sister-in-law. Apparently, I wasn't finding the right buttons to press. She dropped what she was doing, took time out of her busy schedule, and came over. Would I have done the same? Or, would I have reviewed the numerous tasks I had to accomplish that day and found no room for the needs of others? It would probably have been the latter.

She arrived cheery, and eager to work on my computer. She was so earnestly interested in solving the problem. I admired her diligence as she patiently sat down and stared at the peculiar screen of foreign messages. She wrote down the errors word for word.

Of course, her patience was rewarded, and the computer was fixed.

Now why couldn't I do that? Yes, I truly needed help. I decided from that moment on that I would try to slow down, read, think, and pray that I would be blessed with the gift of wisdom and understanding. First and foremost, though, I would try to re-prioritize my life and leave room to respond to the needs of others. I was so grateful for her help—I could only pray that I might have that kind of optimistic hope in finding solutions.

We have to love others on their terms—speak their "love language." I've had the pleasure of reading the book "The Five Love Languages," by Gary Chapman. This book has taught me how to love others the way they need to be loved, not the way I think I ought to love them. For example, if I think cleaning my basement would tell my husband I love him, I'd be kidding myself. Yet, if I paid all the bills, cooked him a wonderful dinner, spoke softly, and eagerly greeted him with a smile when he walked in the door; he'd interpret that as love for him. I, on the other hand, would have felt loved if he had cleaned the basement.

We have a choice to respond energetically or apathetically to those around us. I know very well how hard this is, that's why I pray for God to fill me with His grace and enable me to release my indifference to Him. Together we can achieve great things one step at a time. If we have faith, we can learn from our mistakes and grow.

I was in rare form on Saturday night. Charlie and I were supposed to go out to dinner with our relatives, but I was fed up with the basement remaining in such disarray. I decided to clean it out right then and there. Legally, we are supposed to keep our paperwork for a period of seven years. Well, ours had become a part of the foundation.

Charlie was opening stores at the rate of about one per year, and I was overwhelmed. Our office staff consisted of an off-the-premises bookkeeper, our board of directors (Charlotte & Pudge, our two dogs), and me. Rather than assertively address the issue, I let it get to the point of destruction. I let my anger get the best of me and began ravishing through the debris. Charlie, of course, remained calm and went out to dinner as planned.

The next morning, I woke up with the same determination to finish what I had started. I could have chosen to discuss the problem; but, no, I had to continue ranting and raving as if yelling would make him hear me better. It only caused him to feel belittled. After making his usual phone calls, he left; and I gave up. I quit for the umpteenth time and left. I packed my bags with all my self-help books, and checked into the nearest hotel to educate myself on conflict resolution.

I outlined my thoughts, decided what needed to be done, considered what I was willing to do and had time for, listed my requests, and reviewed applicable Bible verses. Now why couldn't I do that at home when I needed to? I think it was because I was moving so fast that I didn't take time to pray before I responded. Well, the time served me well. After three hours and numerous phone calls with Charlie, I was ready to go home and work it out.

I realized that nothing is worth losing my relationship over. Satan is very tricky and tries to deceive us into believing that issues are more important than people. Well he's wrong. God wants us to value our relationships. I didn't have to flee—God gives us the strength to handle each crisis as it arises. All I had to do was pray for His intervention. When I came home, the basement was clean. Charlie hired my son and his friend to do it under his supervision.

We took time to review my Biblically-based notes. By handling conflict patiently and lovingly, we're able to constructively resolve issues more effectively to everyone's satisfaction. This was a much better solution than how I had initially reacted. I'm sure this situation will arise again in the future. Hopefully, I will deal with it calmly and assertively.

If you believe, you will receive whatever you ask for in prayer."

Mt 21:22

Before we react to any situation or take part in any venture, we can choose to pray. When our plans are committed to the Lord, they'll most certainly succeed in accordance with His will. As we've all heard it said, we can attract more bees with honey than vinegar.

Chapter 5
Anticipating One Another's Needs

My Aunt Natalie was in the hospital recently. She's 85 years old and has been suffering with heart problems. I was telling her about all the times in my life she's made a significant difference. She always makes people feel needed and loved. Almost all my cousins and siblings had their birthday parties and celebrations in her home. She consistently surrounded herself with loved ones. Family and friends flocked to her home to enjoy good food and company.

Aunt Natalie always took time to have fun with us. Housework was never more important than us. She'd teach us how to bake her famous vanilla cookies with the cookie press. We took bubble baths and painted the ceramic figures on the lawn. She'd always come in the pool and swim with us. She never worried about her hair.

We loved having the yearly Easter egg hunt at her home. She never minded when all the kids turned the house upside down looking for the eggs. She let me wash the dishes as a young girl in the tub of sudsy water. At home, I was usually only worthy of drying them.

When I thought about why I loved her so much, I realized that it was because I felt accepted and loved in her presence. She had such an easy way about her and the way she welcomed company. Nothing was ever too much for her. I wanted to be that way. Was I afraid of not being accepted by others? Why was I trying to please everyone else when it was only God that I really had to please? If I only did what was right in His eyes, the rest would fall into place.

> "Whoever has my commandments and obeys them, he is the one that loves me. He that loves me will be loved by my Father, and I too will love him, and show myself to him."
>
> Jn 14:21

In emergencies, we must respond urgently to people's needs, even if it means sacrificing our plans. Charlie told me of a time when he was finishing up work at the butcher shop one night. His family owned and operated the business for forty years, and it was quite successful. They were honored to have served four generations of customers. Charlie knew that his passion for the business caused his grades in college to suffer, but he thought he could balance both well.

That night, he knew he had to study diligently for an exam he was to take the following day. If he didn't study, chances were he'd fail the course. As he was leaving the shop, one of the butchers slashed his leg with a knife while boning out a side of beef. Charlie immediately put the butcher in the car and rushed him to the hospital.

The butcher hardly spoke any English, so Charlie stayed with him at the hospital until he received the necessary medical attention. Needless to say, Charlie failed the test he was supposed to study for. Now that's self-sacrificial love.

I recall many other times when he'd dissolve his plans in order to accommodate someone else's needs. His family had a housekeeper for twenty-three years before she became ill. She, too, needed medical attention one afternoon when we were going out. He quickly put her in his two-seater convertible (which was not very easy as she was somewhat of a heavy-set, older woman), took her to the hospital, and cared for her as he wept with compassion.

When our children were born, I prayed that he would be the one to drive me to the hospital and stay with me because I knew he'd get me there quickly and tend to my needs. I was so cold when Anthony was born. After losing so much body fluid, the nurse wouldn't get a blanket for me because she said they were all in the dryer. I was shivering when he proceeded directly over to the dryer, retrieved a warm blanket, and wrapped me with it. Acts of kindness speak volumes.

I know God wants us to love one another unconditionally. We need to reprioritize in emergencies, and forfeit our own needs and desires in order to help others. By all means we shouldn't become extremists and put out every minor fire. I'm the first to use my answering machine in order to screen the emergencies that come my way. We should pray earnestly for discernment in all things so that we'll know that our priorities are God's priorities.

> "Many people will come and say, 'Come let us go up to the mountain of the Lord, He will teach us His ways, so that we may walk in His paths.' The law will go out from Zion, Jerusalem."
>
> Isaiah 2:3

> "I will instruct you and teach you in the way you should go; I will counsel you and watch over you."
>
> Ps 32:8

Chapter 6
Clearing Away the Clutter

In order for us to remain open and ready for unforeseen circumstances, we need to rid ourselves of the unnecessary clutter in our lives. I realized that most of my stress was being caused by my busy schedule. I could find little time for flexibility, so I decided to let go of a few things I was doing in order to free myself up a bit. When I did this, I was able to experience the blessed free time I was so desperately needing. Sometimes, we have to choose between good, better, and best.

Suddenly, everything I did became more enjoyable. I relished the importance of trivial tasks I previously considered burdensome. Spending the time playing games with my kids, reading, and actually taking the time to understand and apply what it was I read were becoming rewarding solutions to a hectic life. Now I understood why there was a section on job applications for hobbies. If we didn't spend some of our time relaxing, we could quickly become obsessive martyrs.

I was a great martyr. I'd continuously work as if what I did was so significant. Did I need verification that it was important? What was the message I was getting across to others? Wasn't reading important? Wasn't spending quality time with others important? Why did I enjoy my Aunt Natalie's company so much? It was because she made herself available to people. I had to begin choosing to spend my time and energy well.

I was a firm believer in teaching my kids how to handle situations so they would be able to solve problems independently. I didn't mind showing them how a few times; but after the initial lessons, they were expected to handle things like balancing their bank accounts, making doctor appointments, getting referrals, doing laundry, cooking, and other tasks on their own. I was happy to oblige when called upon for advice, but actually doing it was their responsibility.

My goal was to work myself out of a job. We're only enabling people to depend on us more when we do things for them without showing them how to handle it themselves—this is known as learned helplessness. If we continuously handle responsibilities for others, we'll find ourselves being called upon repetitiously for the same issue. We would really be doing ourselves a favor if we would just show others how to accomplish the task on their own.

There's also a sense of satisfaction in having learned something new and accomplishing it independently. My kids feel the same way when they're asked to fix our computer. They want to show us how, so we can do it ourselves the next time without waiting to consult anyone to help us. We're constantly growing and life is full of change. How wonderful it would be if we could approach change with a fearless attitude. If God leads us to it, He'll get us through it. This can be a wonderful opportunity for growth.

My biggest fear is if something happens to Charlie, and I have to take over the businesses. I have been begging him to slow down enough to show me what to do in order to keep the balls in the air. His office is in such disarray; I can't make heads or tails out of anything. Yet he knows exactly where everything is. I do know, though, that if I eliminated all of the clutter in his office, it would help me a great deal in getting started. The situation is in God's hands after that.

We have the opportunity to feel a sense of empowerment when we know what we have and how to find it. It's so much easier when we have less stuff to go through, especially if we don't use most of the things we unnecessarily keep. Just think of the happy recipients of all those wonderful things we donate.

Chapter 7

Forgiveness

> "A man's wisdom gives him patience; it is to his glory to overlook an offense."
>
> Pv 19:11

It's so easy to pick an argument and so difficult to keep peace. Yet peace is what we all strive to achieve in our lives. So why argue? It's usually not worth it for the minor issues; however, the confrontations that need addressing should be handled calmly and assertively with "I feel" statements. For example: "I feel hurt when you speak to me in that tone of voice." This allows the people who are hurt to take ownership of their feelings. It also avoids a defensive attitude in the offender.

Evening is a difficult time for me because I get up so early in the morning. I'm more likely to say something I don't mean late at night as opposed to the morning, when I'm fresh and alert. My family knows better than to ask too much of me at that time or they might be greeted with a character they'd rather not deal with.

I've learned it's best to be flexible when it's not the right time for someone. They might be impatient or irritable for no apparent reason and take it out on the first person that's available. It really helps to overlook these unintentional offenses. They can only lead to heated, insignificant arguments.

I knew that a recent debate I had was quickly escalating into an argument. I could feel the juices inside me begin to boil like lava. Immediate action was necessary. I prayed that God would give me the patience and love I needed to handle the situation.

Charlie and I decided that our three teenagers should carry a credit card on them at all times just in case they ever needed it. We set a thousand dollar limit between the three of them and asked them to use it only in emergencies. Apparently, the word emergencies needed to be redefined.

In addressing the issue, the discussion was quickly getting out of control, so I prayed for guidance and didn't wait to figure out what Jesus would do. This was my first mistake. I knew I had to take away the car keys because I didn't want anyone driving while angry. In retrospect, if I had done what

Jesus would do, I would have waited to discuss the matter when we were all calm. Adding wood to the fire only makes it burn brighter. I also could have called the credit card company to freeze the account. The Holy Spirit reminded me of the quote from Colossians 3:21,

> "Fathers, do not embitter your children, or they will be discouraged."

The next morning, after a two-week grounding sentence was firmly in place, we discussed the matter calmly and rationally. We heard each other out, and we negotiated a fair settlement for everyone. The car and credit card would be unusable for the duration of the sentence; and we would discuss things like mature adults from that moment on.

Future emergency items were written down on a list which, in my definition, did not include cosmetics or anything we already had but were too lazy to look for. Their attitudes changed dramatically. For good behavior, maturity, and a change of heart one week was eliminated from the sentence. They've learned to reconsider their purchases and now understand the meaning of the word "necessity."

The next time a discussion turns into a heated argument, I'll remember to take responsible, immediate action when necessary and discipline in love.

I know better now to wait until everyone is calm to discuss the issue and negotiate a fair solution for all involved. By remaining calm, you ensure that the other person will also remain calm. Moreover, forgiveness and unconditional love both cover a multitude of sins.

Our relationships are so valuable. Jeopardizing them is a stiff price to pay for being right. It's usually not in me to do this gracefully, so I pray for God to intervene and enable me to face each situation with patience, forgiveness, and understanding. When we're in the presence of someone who is constantly bringing up our faults with little or no recognition for our good intentions, we do well in being still and knowing that God will help us.

After all, Jesus was stoned, criticized, ridiculed, betrayed, and killed for no good reason. He will help us through any difficult situation we are put into if we only trust in Him, love and forgive others, and overlook offenses. That's what He meant when He said to turn the other cheek.

> "But I tell you, do not resist an evil person. If someone strikes you on the right cheek, turn to him the other also."
>
> Mt 5:39

This certainly takes a great deal of practice. The juices inside us are sure to be stirred and our old selves will be striving to come through; but it's best to stop, take a deep breath, and hold our tongues. We need time to collect our thoughts and assertively deal with the issue at hand. Our relationships would surely prosper if we all practiced this technique.

As Jesus was dying on the cross he said,

> "Forgive them, Father, for they do not know what they are doing."
>
> Lk 23:34

A good friend at my parish once explained to me that she believed it was too difficult for Jesus to forgive His persecutors. He, too, needed the Father's grace in order to do so.

Chapter 8

Choosing Our Response

We can't control what happens to us in life, but we can control our reaction to it. How many times have we been greeted with surprises we weren't expecting? Whether it was something inappropriate or worrying that was said to us about a situation, we must stop and think of our response and all of the details, which lead up to our reaction to it.

When I've become angry with my children for not telling me where they were going, or for going somewhere I didn't think I said they could go, before I fly off the handle and get upset, I force myself to remember the details of the conversation. If I listened carefully and stopped what I was doing to give them my undivided attention, wouldn't I have heard what they were asking me more clearly? Of course, it helps if they don't tell me while I'm sleeping.

There was a time when I'd just continue my task at hand, but now I know better to stop and pay attention to the person speaking to me. This eliminates so much confusion and conflict. It also makes the person feel respected and heard. Repeating the statement also helps.

Good listening skills are obviously a must in avoiding conflict. I've learned to nod my head, give good eye contact, say "umhm" or "I see" as they speak to me; and then repeat what I understood them to say. I don't think offering my comments, or throwing in a story of my own to support what I've heard helps much. Sometimes just being quiet isn't enough; it's better if we try to actively listen with small words and gestures of acknowledgement.

When I've had a rough day, I don't necessarily want the answers to my problems; I just want to be heard. A generous ear and a shoulder to lean on are all that's necessary to comfort me. If we extend this courtesy to others, we'll see a world of confusion diminish drastically. It's so much easier than trying to solve everyone's problems. We really should leave that cumbersome task to God. He's so much better at it.

Through careful listening and taking ample time to contemplate our response, we can console others with a servant's heart. Rather than come off as being self-righteous, we can view the situation through the eyes of God and ask ourselves, *What would Jesus do?* If we don't consider our reaction, we might just say something we don't mean.

> "Do not let any unwholesome talk come out of your mouths, but only what is helpful for building others up according to their needs, that it may benefit those who listen. And do not grieve the Holy Spirit of God, with whom you were sealed for the day of redemption."
>
> Eph 4:29–30

Chapter 9

Live Each Day As Though It Were Our Last

I was listening to President Bush speak to the press last night. He went on to say how he would fulfill the oath he took with his hand on the Bible, doing everything possible to protect the people of the United States. Saddam Hussein is a world-wide threat and has no regard for his own people let alone others. President Bush indicated how he believed Saddam Hussein would not hesitate to use the chemical weapons he has. He continued to say that our safety is certainly at risk if we choose to ignore his attempts to increase his military capacity.

After witnessing the World Trade Center attacks, I'm most certainly convinced that this is true. Thousands of innocent people were killed on September 11th at the hands of Bin Laden and his brain-washed followers. We do not know if today is our last day here. We must do everything we can to rectify our relationships, repent of our sins, and ask God for His unconditional love and forgiveness. We must pray to our Father in Heaven to fill us with His grace to do His will.

How would we live differently if today were our last day? Why not realize the importance of extending the same love to others that we need from God? Wouldn't that be wonderful? Anger and dissensions would melt away and leave room for joy and peace.

When I go to sleep at night, I think over the events of my day. When I regret what I've said or done and haven't asked for forgiveness, I'm not at peace. On a good day, I can rest easily knowing that I've done the best I could in rectifying my relationships and giving of myself wholeheartedly.

We need to have patience, which is easier said than done. In being patient with ourselves, we permit a peaceful response to develop that is in line with God's will. I'm still struggling with this and constantly pray for God's intervention. When we allow irritating events to accumulate, the last-straw effect comes into play. If we learn to isolate each issue and deal with it assertively, it won't have the chance to escalate into a full-blown argument.

Chapter 10
Keep a Sense of Humor

I've heard it said that "laughter is the best medicine," and I totally agree. Sometimes we just have to drop everything and laugh. If we remain too serious, we fall into the danger of trying to analyze and correct every situation. We could go out of our minds trying to figure everything out. I find it helpful to just laugh.

When we begin to take ourselves too seriously, laughter dissolves the tension. Life is too short to get all caught up in so many little details that really won't matter in the end. I want to see the funny side of things, not always try to understand everything. If we imagine living life through the eyes of a child, we enable our souls to soar to new heights.

"I tell you the truth, unless you change and become like little children, you will never enter the kingdom of heaven. Therefore, whoever humbles himself like this child is the greatest in the kingdom of heaven. And whoever welcomes a little child like this in my name welcomes me."

Mat 16:3–5

The truth is we don't always know why we do the things we do. What matters most is that we're ready to forgive, forget, laugh at and learn from our mistakes, and move on. This is another reason why we need God. He'll help us forgive others and ourselves. If we let Him, He'll fill us with the grace to do this.

One morning, while I was doing the kids' laundry that I told them I wasn't going to do anymore, Nancy came up to me and asked, "Does this skirt look alright? I didn't have time to iron my other one?" She looked the picture of perfection, a mother's dream; but of course, being the perfectionist she is, she wasn't happy.

Soon after, I heard crying in the kitchen. While rushing off to school because her boyfriend was waiting outside, she spilled a cup of tea. She was trying to juggle it with her plate of toast. Was this any reason to cry? She wasn't even late for school but just continued to sob while she mechanically wiped the floor.

To the contrary, after Linda came into the kitchen looking casual and happy in her mismatched sweats.

She began fighting with the plastic wrap after the restaurant-sized box fell to the floor. I know God gives us such different children because He wants us to know how to handle the vast differences we all have. She haphazardly grabbed an old, crumpled lunch bag and stuffed any edible items she could find into it. Linda was totally oblivious to the intricacies that made Nancy upset. You have to laugh or you'll cry.

Chapter 11

Loneliness

One of the most common complaints I hear from older people is that they're so lonely. It's so hard to get used to the solitude when you've had a thriving household all your life. We grow up in an active home and move on to create another of our own. The wonderful feeling of being needed is so familiar, and then it's gone.

How do we go from this lively environment to gracefully embracing old age without feeling lonely? Staying active and close to God is crucial. I often think of the lifestyle of religious people. How do they remain peaceful and content? I truly believe it's by keeping God in their heart every moment and actively doing His will. We cannot expect to be happy when we are wallowing in self pity.

If we seek the face of God in others and in our situations, we'll find fulfillment and security. We went to see the play "Les Miserables." In one of the songs, I was touched to hear the lyrics: "For to love another person is to see the face of God." How profound this statement was to me, and how true.

Remaining active is very important. If we involve ourselves in worthy projects and helping others, we feel purposeful. God has put each one of us here for a reason. We need one another, especially for those gifts and talents in which we differ. Psalm 139 reminds us how we are all fearfully and wonderfully made.

> "O Lord, You have searched me and You know me. You know when I sit and when I rise; You perceive my thoughts from afar. You discern my going out and my lying down; You are familiar with all my ways. Before a word is on my tongue You know it completely, O Lord. You hem me in—behind and before; You have laid Your hand upon me. Such knowledge is too wonderful for me, too lofty for me to attain.

> "Where can I go from Your Spirit? Where can I flee from Your presence? If I go up to the heavens, You are there; if I make my bed in the depths, You are there. If I rise on the wings of the dawn, if I settle on the far side of the sea, even there

Your hand will guide me, Your right hand will hold me fast. If I say, 'Surely the darkness will hide me and the light become night around me,' even the darkness will not be dark to You; the night will shine like the day, for darkness is as light to You.

"For You created my inmost being; You knit me together in my mother's womb. I praise You because I am fearfully and wonderfully made; Your works are wonderful, I know that full well. My frame was not hidden from You when I was made in the secret place. When I was woven together in the depths of the earth, Your eyes saw my unformed body. All the days ordained for me were written in Your book before one of them came to be. How precious to me are Your thoughts, O God. How vast is the sum of them! Were I to count them, they would outnumber the grains of sand.

"When I awake, I am still with You. If only You would slay the wicked, O God! Away from me, you bloodthirsty men! They speak of You with evil intent; Your adversaries misuse Your name. Do I not hate those who hate You, O Lord, and abhor those who rise up against You? I have nothing but hatred for them; I count them my enemies. Search me, O God, and know my heart, test me and know my anxious thoughts. See if there is any offensive way in me, and lead me in the way everlasting."

Romans 12:4–6 shows how we are one body with many parts.

"Just as each of us has one body with many members, and these members do not all have the same function, so in Christ we who are many form one body, and each member belongs to all the others. We have different gifts according to the grace given us."

When I teach class at my parish, it's never easy for me to break away from what I have to do. However, when I'm there, I'm fulfilled from the curiosity I find in the children. We learn more about God and take time to discuss any ideas, thoughts, and questions the kids have. It's truly an enlightening experience. A friend of mine, who is a widow, decided to teach with me, and she loves it.

We must be careful not to let our natural impulses cause us to be pessimistic. Seeking out the good in situations as well as in people is the key to peace, happiness, and fulfillment. Don't let Satan gain any ground here. Be optimistic and know that God is always with us. If we trust Him to show us our gifts and talents, He'll reveal opportunities for us to help others. Pray constantly for wisdom and discernment. Then, take the plunge by enjoying the fruits of your labor.

I keep the following guidelines tacked onto the wall in front of my desk and read them when I'm feeling lonely.

Seven Basic Guidelines for a Happy and Meaningful Life

1. Commit yourself daily to the purpose of glorifying Jesus Christ.
2. Spend some time each day to meditating on God's word and applying it to your life.
3. Get rid of grudges daily.
4. Spend a little time each day getting more intimate with your mate and children. Parents, brothers, sisters, and other close relatives should also have a high priority. Do all you can to resolve conflicts. Don't ever seek vengeance on people. Do the best you can and leave the rest up to God.
5. Spend some time each week having fellowship and fun with at least one or two committed Christian friends of the same sex. If you are married, have fun with other married couples. In this way, husband and wife can together benefit from intimacy with others.
6. Be involved in a daily routine (including work, play, housework, projects) that brings personal satisfaction to you. Be convinced

that this routine is God's will and purpose for your life—your way of glorifying Him.
7. Do something nice for one special person each week. This kind deed can be physical (helping with a chore, for example), emotional (buying a book or giving counsel), or spiritual (having devotions together).

These ideas really help me to know God's will for my life. We need to pray for His grace to intercede and help us find our calling. If we give one another the companionship we long for when we're faced with loneliness, we won't feel driven to seek it in the wrong places. We all want to be loved, and it's in giving that we receive. When we show love for others, love will be returned to us abundantly. The rewards are immeasurable.

Chapter 12
All We Need Is Love

I recall a story I read in a spiritual book about a priest whose frustration was trying to clean up a street in front of his church. There were prostitutes walking up and down the street advertising their services. The people tried picketing, yelling, belittling, protesting, and passing out flyers. Nothing seemed to penetrate through to them to stop what they were doing.

The priest came up with a bright idea. He and his parishioners invited each one of the prostitutes in for coffee, tea, and quiet conversation in which the priest and the parishioners did most of the listening. They found out the women's birthdays and remembered them with small gestures to celebrate and made them feel important.

Soon, they came to realize that the priest and his parishioners were good, decent, caring individuals. They realized how good it felt to be treated with respect and wanted to be more like the people helping them. One at a time, they each changed their lifestyle. This was done with love.

I remember the reading at our wedding ceremony from 1Corinthians 13:4–13:

> "Love is patient, love is kind, it does not envy, it does not boast, it is not proud. It is not rude, it is not self-seeking, it is not easily angered, it keeps no record of wrongs. Love does not delight in evil but rejoices with the truth. It always protects, always trusts, always perseveres. Love never fails."

We need to love the sinner and hate the sin. Is it really worth losing our relationships with the people we love over our choice to sin? As Jesus proved to the woman caught in adultery:

> "When they kept on questioning Him, He straightened up and said to them, 'If any one of you is without sin, let him be the first to throw a stone at her.' Again He stooped down and wrote on the ground.
>
> "At this, those who heard began to go away one at a time, the older ones first, until only Jesus was

left, with the woman still standing there. Jesus straightened up and asked her 'Woman, where are they? Has no one condemned you?'

"'No one, sir,' she said.

"'Then neither do I condemn you,' Jesus declared. 'Go now and leave your life of sin.'"

Jn 8:7–11

The Bible states in Matthew 7:3–5 :

"Why do you look at the speck of sawdust in your brother's eye and pay no attention to the plank in your own eye? How can you say to your brother, 'Let me take the speck out of your eye,' when all the time there is a plank in your own eye? You hypocrite, first take the plank out of your own eye, and then you will see clearly to remove the speck from your brother's eye."

If we know that our actions are clearly sin according to God's Word, we must remember that forgiveness is always available to us. We need to repent, ask for forgiveness, and change our lifestyle by walking in obedience to God's will. We can try to lovingly persuade others through living a righteous life. The consequences of our choices will teach us valuable lessons. God has blessed us with the gift of free will. In accepting God's forgiveness, we can rest assured He will give us the grace to change.

> "If you hold to my teaching, you are really my disciples. Then you will know the truth, and the truth will set you free."
>
> Jn 8:31–32

When our children defy us and do things against our wishes, we still love them. Raising three teenagers has been no easy task. Mood swings run rampant throughout our home. Whenever we discover that one of our children has not been the angel we thought them to be, we don't excommunicate them. How would we be able to influence them? We ask God for the grace to love them unconditionally.

If we reach up to God, He will give us the strength to love others unconditionally. Without Him this would be a great struggle. When people feel loved, they are able to hear better.

> "If I speak in the tongues of men and of angels, but have not love, I am only a resounding gong or a clanging cymbal."
>
> 1Cor 13:1

Chapter 13

Get Rid of Grudges Daily

"He who covers over an offense promotes love, but whoever repeats the matter separates close friends."

Pr 17:9

Have you ever tried to talk to a person who becomes easily offended? It's like walking through a minefield trying to avoid an explosion. It's difficult to be in their company because you don't know what to say or how to say it without making them blow up. If we mostly overlook ridiculous remarks, we will be a great deal happier for it.

We can't force people to do anything they don't want to do; and even if we do, how much could we truly get out of the experience if it isn't genuine? I pray every day for the grace to be able to overlook offenses since, I'm sure, I also dish them out. I find it so much easier when I recite the Lord's prayer:

> "Our Father, who art in heaven, hallowed be thy name, thy kingdom come, thy will be done, on earth, as it is in heaven. Give us this day our daily bread, forgive us our trespasses as we forgive those who trespass against us.
>
> "And lead us not into temptation but deliver us from evil."
>
> Mt 6:1–8

When I recall my trespasses, and the offenses I've given to others, I find it so much easier to overlook those offenses intentionally or unintentionally directed toward me. God will give us the strength we need for each new day. I'm sure that's why He designed the days of the week.

> "Do not let the sun go down while you are still angry, and do not give the devil a foothold."
>
> Eph 4:26–27

Think of how many arguments we could avoid if we only got rid of our bitterness daily. Every night when I go bed, I pray that I have not taken offense or withheld forgiveness from anyone who might have hurt me. I try to apologize to anyone whom I

Get Rid of Grudges Daily

might have offended in any way. I've heard it said that forgiveness is a gift we give to ourselves. If we don't give and accept this gift, bitterness will infect our souls and rob our joy.

Rather than become bitter, I pray to God that He'll help me release these arduous situations to Him. In knowing my own faults, I find it so much easier to forgive others. We need to remember the good things people do and not the bad. Most of the time, they don't even know they've hurt us.

> "Get rid of all bitterness, rage and anger, brawling and slander, along with every form of malice. Be kind and compassionate to one another, forgiving each other just as in Christ God forgave you."
> Eph 4:31–32

Chapter 14

Trust Him

On a business trip Charlie and I went on, we sat through many seminars. We were delighted to hear a guest speaker tell his story. His name was Gene Kranz, and he was the flight director of Apollo 13. Mr. Kranz is the author of the book "Failure Is Not an Option."

During lunch, he described the intricate story of his team's mission to assist the Apollo 13 flight crew in returning home safely from space. It was a very suspenseful story in which he and his team tried to turn around an unsuccessful attempt to land on the moon. When Apollo 13 was about to enter the earth's atmosphere, Kranz had a gut feeling that he should instruct the crew to attempt entry in a way that was contrary to what most of the team believed. It was at that point that he said:

"We must do everything we can, and then hand it over to a higher authority."

The group of people working on this mission including Mr. Kranz, I'm sure, would be considered geniuses. They must be among the most learned individuals in their field. I was so impressed that people of this capacity of intelligence would feel confident in admitting that a higher authority not only exists, but also would helps us in dire need.

The team motto was "Trust, Leadership, Teamwork, and Values." I'm sure God wants us to incorporate each one of these aspects into our daily lives. Gene Kranz was able to do just that with his team of professionals by following a gut feeling, which I believe is the Holy Spirit guiding us. After they did everything they could, they trusted God to guide them in the solution.

We can show our trust in God in so many ways. On our flight home from Orlando, one of the passengers was with a high-spirited group. Before the flight took off, she did the sign of the cross and blessed herself, I'm sure praying for a safe flight as most of us do. I later learned that she was a flight attendant. It was refreshing to discover that she had so much trust in God; which takes the form of us trusting one another—as in trusting the pilot.

Consider the aspects of our lives in which we must trust others. It must be that God wants it that way because not only does He tell us in the Bible, but also we can't function well without trusting Him to work in others. He promised to send the Holy Spirit to help us. The Spirit comes to us in various ways including the form of trust and instinct. Don't ignore this wonderful friend we need for wisdom and discernment.

> "If you had responded to my rebuke, I would have poured out my heart to you and made my thoughts known to you."
>
> Pv 1:23

> "And I will ask the Father, and He will give you another Counselor to be with you forever—the Spirit of truth. The world cannot accept Him because it neither sees Him or knows Him. But you know Him, for He lives with you and will be in you."
>
> Jn 14:16–17

> "And I will put My Spirit in you, and move you to follow my decrees and be careful to keep my laws."
>
> Eze 36:27

> "As for you, the anointing you received from Him remains in you and you do not need anyone to teach you. But as His anointing teaches you about all things and as that anointing is real, not

> counterfeit—just as it has taught you, remain in Him."
>
> 1Jn 2:27

With God's help, we can overcome any evil thoughts or actions that tempt us. We must exercise our free will and choose to do what is right and just. He will give us the strength we need to excel. All we have to do is trust in Him. It's not necessary for us to understand how.

When we drive our car, do we know how it operates before we drive it? Not usually, we just drive and trust in the fact that it will take us to our destination. It's the same way with God. If we only trust in His almighty power to lead us, He'll guide us to wherever He needs us to be. He knows exactly what He needs us to experience in order to be humbled.

> "Trust in the Lord with all your heart and lean not on your own understanding; in all your ways acknowledge Him, and He will make your paths straight."
>
> Pr 3:5–6

In order for God to help us, we must submit our will to Him. Especially when we know we cannot break a habit or an addiction on our own. He wants us to come to Him like little children trusting in Him to help us change. He will supply all of our needs in order for us to heal. We don't need to understand how; we just need to pray for faith that will move mountains. He'll do the rest. God only needs our will to let Him in to do His work within us.

> "For it is by grace you have been saved, through faith and this not from yourselves, it is the gift of God."
>
> Eph 2:8

> "'Have faith in God,' Jesus answered. I tell you the truth, if anyone says to this mountain, 'Go, throw yourself into the sea, and does not doubt in his heart but believes that what he says will happen, it will be done for him.'"
>
> Mk 11:22–23

I recently had to admit my daughter to the hospital. I knew she'd be there for quite a while. What could have been a long and arduous process became a peaceful and constructive experience.

While there, I encountered a woman in the hospital who was suffering through the same chronic illness. She was being admitted for the third time. She went on to explain how the illness has consumed her and it became bigger than anything in her life. I felt the Holy Spirit work through me when I responded: "Nothing we can face is bigger than God."

Chapter 15

Harmony in Nature

I love to take a walk as often as possible. It's such a special time for me to collect my thoughts and hand them all over to God. Whether I'm alone (with God, of course), or in the pleasure of someone's company, I thoroughly enjoy getting in tune with nature. There's something about the woods that speak to me in the form of God's beautiful creation.

While I'm walking, I look all around me and try to find the hidden meaning in God's artwork. For instance, when I look at the trunks of the enormous trees, I see the foundation of years and years of growth. I allow my eye to stray along the branches and realize that we are very much like these trees.

Primarily, we're all reaching up to God; but, like the branches, we're all worshiping in our own way with a common goal in mind. Some branches reach straight up while others branch out to the right or left. One enormous branch actually spread out from the base of the tree along the ground then up toward heaven. A walkway was built around it.

I realize that we're all diverse individuals and worship God in various ways. We can celebrate our differences and remember that even though we're all different, we all bleed the same color red. As I walk along the path, I see small animals roaming, hear the lovely song of birds chirping, and bask in the symphonic sounds of nature.

I'm amazed at the constancy of the slow growth process that surrounds me. It's incredible how the ice and snow melt away permitting the new seeds to flourish. To me, the ice and snow symbolize the cold, hard trials we struggle through. The soil provides the nutrients for a healthy life to cultivate. Our hearts are similar to the soil. If we allow God to work through us, and we become good soil, His omnipotent love will germinate. If we will decrease, He will increase.

I love the way the old, fallen tree trunks are used as steps to bring us to a higher place. This represents a fallen people who have the compassion to help others who are suffering with similar problems—hopefully bringing them to a better place. When I stop on the bridge, I study the flowing water over the rocks.

Harmony in Nature

From my perspective, the rocks are a symbol of God's strength and stability. I see the water as life's battles flowing around and over them transforming into a cleansing experience.

> "He must become greater; I must become less."
> Jn 3:30

One day, when I started out walking in the sunshine, the weather slowly gave way to rain. I love the rain because it makes me feel refreshed as it replenishes the environment. It reminds me that God cleanses us of our sins and makes us new again. Nature drinks in the well-needed water utilizing its revitalizing benefits. If we open our hearts to God's love and drink in His goodness, He'll perform His marvelous work in and through us. Then we can exult in His presence.

I realized after taking various routes on these nature trails, that each trail led me deeper into the woods; but all ultimately led me out again to civilization. This represented a sign that we must take time to retreat; and then bring our peace back out into the world. Even Jesus needed forty days in the desert. Let's welcome each new day as a gift of time, and may the result of our actions be fruitful and pleasing to God.

"A farmer went out to sow his seed. As he was scattering the seed, some fell along the path; it was trampled on, and the birds of the air ate it up. Some fell on rock, and when it came up, the plants withered because they had no moisture. Other seed fell among thorns, which grew up with it and choked the plants. Still other seed fell on good soil. It came up and yielded a crop, a hundred times more than was sown. He who has ears to hear, let him hear."

Lk 8:5–8

I pray that God will transform our hearts into fertile soil so that we may produce an abundant crop of good works, loving kindness, forgiveness, and compassion.

Chapter 16

Detachment

Nancy knocked on my bedroom door just before bedtime with tears flowing down her face. She anxiously said,

"Mommy, did you see the ring Chris gave me outside on the patio table?"

"No, I haven't."

"He's going to be so upset with me. I don't know where it is—I know I left it there!"

"Nancy, come in here for a minute. I want to talk to you about possessions," I said as I patted the chair I was sitting on.

She plopped herself down on my double-wide chaise lounge and comfortably lay her head on my chest as I hugged her, stroking her arm gently.

"Please know that whatever God chooses to bless us with in this life should be used and enjoyed; but we cannot let ourselves feel hopeless without it."

"But Mommy, I feel so irresponsible and careless."

"Why don't you call him and ask him if he's seen it? I'm sure he's waiting for your call to see if you even noticed it was missing."

"I'm so afraid he's going to be mad at me." Her guilt overwhelmed her.

"Do you see this wedding ring on my finger?" I pointed out. "This is my third wedding band. The first one was temporary, and I lost the second one. We simply can't get too attached to our belongings. We most certainly can appreciate the symbols they represent, but becoming too attached to them will only detract from our attachment to God. They cannot promise us peace, security, and fulfillment—only God can provide us with that.

"Think of the poor people in the Holocaust. Their families and possessions were taken away from them, but no one can take away our souls. We all work so hard for everything we have, but when we place our faith in our belongings, we're putting our hope in empty promises. Our vision is so clouded that we no longer see what's truly important—each other.

"When we offer all of our work up to God in worship of Him, He blesses us with satisfaction, contentment, and fulfillment. We don't need the praise of people or materialistic gains when we have

God's approval. Suddenly, we're no longer concerned with competition but only in doing our work in the best way we can to please God."

"I think I'll go call Chris now. Thanks, Mommy—I'll remember what you told me."

I prayed for her that night and for so many of us who fruitlessly seek our fulfillment in material things. In remaining thankful to God for our blessings, we can worship Him rather than the things we possess. Moreover, in detaching ourselves from our possessions, we can clearly see from whom we derive our strength.

Our omnipotent God gives us the energy necessary to achieve success. We have that innate drive before we obtain our possessions. The truth of that success lies in knowing we've steered our ambition toward worshiping Him. The fruits of our labor should be enjoyed and shared. In doing so we detach ourselves from them and clearly emulate the giver.

Later that evening, Nancy came back into my room. Smiling gently she said,

"Mommy, I spoke to Chris. He took my ring inside for me. I told him I was frantic over losing it, but there's nothing we can ever buy that's more important than our relationship with God and one another."

Chapter 17

Discerning Interruptions

I was a well-programmed machine, as I raced through my day trying to get as many things done as possible. *I hope no one bothers me today; I have so much to do,* I thought. My in-box was filled to capacity, and I knew it would be several consecutive days of working before I'd see daylight. Charlie and I worked feverishly for the past twelve years and have expanded our business from one restaurant to eighteen—give or take the mistakes along the way. I desperately thought, *how did life get this hectic? I have no time to think about it. Contemplating is a luxury I have no time to indulge in.* I encouraged myself to just keep going—slowing down would be a crime. When we opened our first restaurant, I promised myself I would only handle accounts payable. I did'nt want to take too much attention away from our three children. Every day brought a new set of problems, and I quickly became the substitute for the daily "no-shows."

In the interim, I'd bring my kids, all under the age of three, to work with me. Charlie began bringing home housekeepers, and we consecutively interviewed over thirteen. I found fault with almost all of them because I hated to relinquish the most important privilege of raising our children to a stranger. I also wanted to teach our children to be responsible for their chores—not depend on someone else to do them.

Charlie was raised by a housekeeper all his life. Going back to work was what my father-in-law conveniently referred to as "therapy;" and my mother-in-law made it clear that she didn't want to be "stuck at home." Society creates this pretty package to entice us with. Many people view homemaking as trivial work that's not prestigious enough to be considered rewarding.

However, every woman is not the same. Each of us is created uniquely by God with specific gifts. Our children are a blessing that God entrusts us with, and raising them to love and worship Him is our highest calling as parents. We're given the opportunity to shape their thoughts and mold their character.

Sadly, I let my faith go on the wayside right after we were married. I foolishly chose not to ask Charlie to go to church with me. He was already so busy, and I didn't want to add any more things to his hectic schedule. I allowed the restlessness of our children to be the excuse that kept me from going as well. I was only fooling myself into believing a lie. If only I realized that God respects our free will and eagerly waits for us to invite Him into our lives, my burdens could have been lifted up—enabling me to find my strength in Him.

This struggle became too difficult to juggle. In one of my weaker moments, I agreed to leave our children with housekeeper number thirteen. *At least they didn't lock her in the basement and run around like they had another,* I reasoned. I decided to go to the office at the store, which would allow me to avoid the many interruptions I had at home.

At that time, Charlie was expanding at the rate of one store per year, in spite of my pleas to deal with what we already had. Of course, the need for help grew like the plague. I began driving to the furthest stores after dropping off the kids at school. I reassured myself that I'd be back in time to see them when they came home from school. But traffic or delays of some other kind would frequently cause me to break my promises.

Did I really have to do this? I know I could save money and work from home. Am I letting society dictate my values? I knew it was time to take a stand. Life became a quest of running from one store to another putting out endless fires. I was tired of giving my kids a vast array of excuses as to why I was always late or absent from their lives. No matter how much I accomplished in a day, I still felt empty and fruitless.

I was headed on a downward spiral to despair. My problems progressively became worse and my physical, emotional, and spiritual health suffered extensively. I pleaded with God for His mercy. *God, I feel so alone and abandoned, even though family and friends surround me. I can't live my life without You. Please help me become obedient to Your calling. Show me how to invite You back into my life.* I opened my Bible to 1 John 3:21–22:

> "Dear friends, if our hearts do not condemn us, we have confidence before God and receive from Him anything we ask, because we obey His commands and do what pleases Him."

I promised God I would replace all my destructive habits with service to Him. I had to walk in obedience and prioritize my schedule according to God's will. We began by going back to church as a family. *The family that prays together stays together*, I reminded myself often. I brought my office work home and only did it when the kids were at school. This enabled me to make myself completely available to them at the end of their school day.

We played sports together, went on picnics in the park, and reveled in each other's company. I read the Bible voraciously, kept a daily journal, held a Bible study in our home, and taught children about God. I was suddenly aware of God's presence all around me. It was there all along for me to recognize, but I was too busy to notice how much I needed Him.

I dismissed our housekeeper and started teaching the kids about time management and responsibility. Each night, I'd print up an hourly schedule for the next day, which allowed me to evaluate my priorities. Our chores became more fun when we did them together. We focused on the benefits of doing them, not what they were keeping us from. Our home is a blessing and caring for it a privilege.

We all developed hands-on experience in life skills; and, in doing so, awakened our appreciation for the vibrant life all around us. If any motivation was necessary, I'd pay the kids for any extra work they did above and beyond their chores. We're willing to pay strangers, so why shouldn't we pay our kids? Are they any less deserving of a reward for their effort? If they don't do as good a job as we expect them to, we can always decrease the pay.

Life is full of interruptions. I know that some can be false temptations to indulge in Satan's lies; but others may be bearers of God's grace. Perhaps they ask us to reconsider our priorities. After considering them with wisdom and discernment, they can become a bridge in our relationships, offering us opportunities to serve God through serving one another. We're reminded of this in 1 Corinthians 10:24:

> "No one should be looking out for his own interests, but for the interests of others."

As a result of this new lifestyle, I'm now the more well-balanced, fulfilled person God has designed me to be. I'm not overwhelmed by guilt and exhaustion, and I'm eager to engage in activities that previously felt frivolous. Like our Lord's mother, Mary, we can learn to say "yes" when God is calling us. If we wait for a convenient moment, we might miss out on all that God has planned for our lives.

Chapter 18

Abandoning Our Vices

Our vices are the crutches we yearn for when we crave comfort from the wrong sources. Our allegiance to them always deceives us by their false ability to pacify us. They tempt us with a temporary satisfaction that quickly dissolves like chocolate in heat as we try to outrun our addiction to them. We permit them to pollute our bodies, minds, and souls with venomous promises of rescue.

As I dust the pictures on Charlie's desk, I recall my tumultuous pain. If pictures could talk, they might tell a much sadder story than the images they portray. On the outside, I looked great—on the inside, I was doomed; and bulimia was my vice.

This road was familiar to me. I traveled it often when I was a young girl of thirteen to about age fifteen. As a young child, I was an easy target for verbal insults. The names I was called played over and over again in my head like a scratched CD. I could feel their fiery darts ripping through my tender soul, freshly opening the wounds as I bled again.

At thirteen the pressure of meeting boys lay heavily on my heart. I ran to my shelter of food for comfort. With bulimia seducing me, I dropped thirty pounds in just under two months.

At thirty the demands of starting our own business, raising our family, and caring for our home were overwhelming. Rather than reaching out to God, once again, I foolishly empowered food to be the idol I worshiped; and the ferocious spiral began to lure me into its turmoil. Why is it that when we don't know what to do, we do what we say we never will? I guess the saying is true that old habits die hard.

I was great at beginning diets, I had done it so often; but keeping them was the problem. I had learned to be comforted by the daily ritual of binging and purging. It silently lubricated my wounds without judgment or criticism. Satan's lies were revealed in these tempting packages as they alienated me from the truth in my life. I had to assertively learn to confront difficult issues, not escape them.

Right after I had done this damage to myself, I couldn't wait to purge so I could rid myself of all those poisonous calories. The ritual fooled me into thinking I could cleanse myself internally, like the sins I had committed would flush away—then I could try again.

The harsh reality of this craft was that the more I rehearsed it, the more I craved to refuel. The emptiness and nutritional imbalance caused a ravenous appetite within me. I allowed this vicious cycle to consume me. My family knew about this ghost that resided within me; but they were helpless, as I didn't even admit I had a problem. I thought I could be everything to everyone.

Evil possesses our souls like a lion its prey, and it rips us apart until we become the living dead. Things beyond our control are meant for the Lord. I was too busy for God. I pushed Him out of my life like teenagers tune out their parents. Why was I letting vanity control me? Was killing myself worth the price in trying to meet the world's standard for beauty?

Once again, I was possessed by this demon. This time from the age of thirty to about thirty six. Sadly, I felt more like sixty-five. My bone structure was visible, and my self-esteem was nowhere to be found. Why do people pay more attention to you when you looked good? Are these the kind of people I respected and wanted to know?

Our family took a trip to Niagara Falls one spring. I was lost in awesome wonder at the power that roared over the falls in God's artwork. I was astounded by the fact that a large portion of the power of the falls was being used for energy. *Could God place that energy in me?* I thought hopefully.

I felt the Holy Spirit in the foaming mist exploding from the falls as if God were trying to touch me. I needed only to open my eyes, ears, and heart to Him, repent, and give Him my will. On that peaceful afternoon, I found God. I was pathetically helpless as I prayed for His merciful intervention.

God, please forgive me for not seeking Your help sooner. I've turned to idols rather than You. Life without Your Spirit is like riding an abandoned carousel. If I become the pipe, will You be the omnipotent water of life that flows through me? I begged. I was so tired of robbing myself of the happiness I knew was in store for me. *I put all of my hope in You, dear Lord; and I know I can trust in Your mercy and healing.*

I made a pact with God to walk in obedience and knew that He would help me. I was sure He would keep His end of the bargain, but would I keep mine? It was time for me to receive the gift of God's grace, pick up my cross, and start walking. I knew in my heart that He would help me, even if I couldn't help myself.

I became a fountain of hope. Every time I had the urge to gorge, I'd give my time to our Lord. I've heard it said that He gives us the precious gift of time, and how we spend that time is our gift back to Him. I'd spend time with our Lord in praise and worship every day. In addition to scheduled prayer time, I'd read and host a Bible study in my home, teach Sunday school, and attend spiritual classes. The more I learned, the more I realized the magnitude of God's kingdom. This journey would take a lifetime of faith, hope, and trust.

I meditated on Ephesians 4:22–24.

> "You were taught with regard to your former way of life, to put off your old self, which is being corrupted by its deceitful desires; to be made new in the attitude of your minds; and to put on the new self, created to be like God in true righteousness and holiness."

When we find ourselves nibbling at Satan's bait, we don't wake up one day and say to ourselves: *Today, I'm going to become a bulimic, an alcoholic, an adulteress, a gambler, or a drug addict.* Continually choosing to sin in bite-sized pieces will stir the tide until it becomes a whirlpool of destruction sucking us in deeper and deeper. If we let them, our vices can devour our souls like cancer unless we choose to reach for our loving and forgiving God. He's bigger than any of our addictions.

> "This is the verdict: Light has come into the world, but men loved darkness instead of light because their deeds were evil. Everyone who does

> evil hates the light, and will not come into the light for fear that his deeds will be exposed. But whoever lives by the truth comes into the light, so that it may be seen plainly that what he has done has been done through God."
>
> Jn 3:19–21

Although it was tough to abandon the refuge my vice offered, turning to Christ came easily. He is my strength. I realize my worth in Him. Psalm 139 convinces us that we are fearfully and wonderfully made. I realized that when I choose to sin, I'm pounding another nail into Jesus' flesh. He sacrificed His life on the cross in order to cleanse us from our sins; and we are not only forgiven but also healed in His name. His body became the bridge to our Father in heaven.

I needed to understand that a lot of people were willing to help me. Like Jesus, I needed to learn to accept their help, and move on.

> "As they led Him away, they seized Simon from Cyrene, who was on his way in from the country, and put the cross on him and made him carry it behind Jesus."
>
> Lk 23:26

If I fell, I quickly confessed my sins and found my courage in our Father in heaven. After repenting with a sincere heart, we have the opportunity to begin again.

Abandoning Our Vices

> "Forget the former things; do not dwell on the past. See, I am doing a new thing. Now it springs up; do you not perceive it?"
>
> Isa 43:18

I'm amazed at what God has done for me. I assist Charlie, our children, and our staff in running our restaurants and have gone back to college—developing an earnest interest in writing and reading inspirational books and articles. Along with my three teenage children, we manage the responsibilities in our home and have personally grown. Where I had thought my shame would be the veil in my relationship with my family, it has only bonded us closer together. God always brings good out of suffering. His glory will always shine through.

I love this new thing God is doing in me, and I can feel my heart soar. The next time we long to indulge in our vices, let's replace those idols with the love and mercy of God. He is waiting for us with open arms and will provide us with all that we need.

Our weaknesses can become a bridge to Him and others rather than a canyon. In abandoning our vices and willingly seeking Him first, we can put all our faith, hope, and trust in God. He will most certainly see us through.

Chapter 19

Suffering Well

The guidance counselor at my daughter's junior high school called me on my cell phone one day.

"Your daughter doesn't want to live anymore," she stated plainly.

The words echoed in my ears as the tears welled up in my eyes and began to roll down my cheeks. I didn't know how to respond.

"I'll be right there to pick her up." I declared.

When I arrived, Linda looked too old for a young girl of thirteen. It seemed as though she was carrying the weight of the world on her shoulders. She looked so sad and helpless.

"What would you suggest I do?" I pleaded.

"I would try art therapy," the guidance counselor mentioned routinely. "It seems to be the latest therapy for children," she went on.

The latest therapy for children? How many children needed therapy, and what was this world coming to? The questions flooded my mind like rolling rapids of white water.

We went to numerous psychiatrists. As per their suggestions, we tried various medications. The side effects for some of them were actually worse than the depression itself. Linda fainted, gained thirty pounds, shivered, and vomited as a result of them.

The school suggested I put her into special education classes. This was completely inappropriate for her since she was doing very well academically. She looked at me with pleading, tear-filled eyes and said, "Mommy, would you please home-school me?"

I was at a loss for words. How could I home-school her? I wasn't a teacher. I only took a few courses in college; but with only fifteen credits under my belt, I wasn't qualified to teach someone, was I?

I thought about Jesus. He held no degrees, didn't have a fancy job or title, and I'm sure he wasn't making a six-figure income. I begged God for an answer. When it finally came to me, no one supported my decision to home-school her.

The doctors, board of education, and even Charlie all disagreed with this solution. However,

I knew God was calling us to rely on Him. I was certain that faith had to be the foundation of the healing process.

Linda was home-schooled for her eighth-grade year. She proved herself to be self-motivated, independent, diligent, and responsible. Not only did she go off all medication, but she was also able to prosper in her faith. We cultivated a deeper relationship with our Lord in our prayer life and came to depend on Him as our source of strength.

When she went back to high school for her ninth-grade year, she made the honor role, began running track, joined the youth group at our parish and her school, and is currently helping people with special needs. She has even developed a following in teaching piano to children as a community service, which eventually prospered into an occupation.

When we're faced with arduous circumstances in our lives, we can reach out to God for coping skills. When we choose to hope in God, we can rest assured in the fact that He hears our cry for help. God didn't promise us that we wouldn't suffer, but He did promise us that He'd always be with us when we do.

When trials come our way, we needn't be overwhelmed with despair; we need only turn to God for comfort. Suffering with Him is knowing that His compassion will help us through any trial. When

Jesus went into the Garden of Gethsemane, He surrendered himself into the hands of His Father. He was able to trust in His Father's love even through desperate situations.

> "Going a little farther, He fell with his face to the ground and prayed, 'My father, if it is possible, may this cup be taken from me. Yet not as I will, but as You will.'"
>
> Mt 26:39

We must stand firm in our time of trial and turn our lives over to the Father. Even Jesus fell several times when carrying His cross. Simon of Cyrene helped Him bear the load. We must help one another, for it is in doing so that we are helping Christ. I recall the song, "Whatsoever you do to the least of My people, that you do unto Me."

If we shoulder our responsibilities with a joyful attitude, we are displaying our hope that God will never give us more than we can handle together. Looking at our situation optimistically, we see the opportunity for growth in fortitude and compassion even in the midst of suffering. Every trial we go through is a humbling experience in which we can learn something by becoming better people.

I consider these devastating circumstances warning signals for us to change our ways and learn to lean on God. He is the potter, and we are the clay.

Only He knows how to shape and mold us into what He needs us to be.

Jesus endured excruciating pain without complaint. In the midst of suffering, we must remember to be faithful. God's healing love is the balm for our wounds. He can make good come out of terrible situations. Think about how on September 11th our world came together and helped one another. The strength to do that was God's grace interceding. We need to lean on Him, and He will always pull us through these trying times.

God will give us the wisdom we need—He is with us every step of the way helping to bear our burdens. We can be comforted in knowing that His strength is available to us. He lives inside every one of us; we need only allow His strength to increase and our despair to decrease. We can be encouraged by the words in Proverbs 15:15:

> "A cheerful look brings joy to the heart, and good news gives health to the bones."

Our behavior usually follows our thought process. If we are thinking negatively, most likely we will act negatively. By filling our minds with positive thoughts, we're able to behave in ways that are more conducive to encouraging others, and ourselves, which, in turn, honor God.

When we endure injustices, Jesus can identify with our persecutions. God will nourish us in our time of need even in the midst of hardships and suffering. Even in our darkest hour, we can, like Jesus, speak words of forgiveness and trust:

> "Father, forgive them for they do not know what they are doing."
>
> Lk 23:34

We walk securely with God by our side feeling our pain. In sharing our rigorous trials with God, we come to realize that we can do ordinary things in extraordinary ways.

By making God a priority in our lives, our trials might not lessen or be eliminated; but by sharing our fears and seeking His help, we invite Him into our minds, hearts, and souls. Through the promptings we receive, He will send the Holy Spirit to direct our conscience toward Him. By accepting our situations on God's behalf, we're enabling Him to be a part of our lives and help us to carry our cross.

From the manger to the cross, Jesus lived in flesh and blood as each one of us does. He knows our pain and can teach us how to suffer well. He powerfully influenced the world positively through His suffering and has not asked the Father why, but has proven to us that He will never leave us.

God speaks to us in silence and through our daily circumstances. He has also provided us with many vehicles for His word such as music, scripture, creation, prayer, books, and faithful family and friends.

Amazing things can happen when we quiet that pessimistic voice within us and listen to His call. He offers us life, light, and love. We need only take in His marvelous gifts and receive soothing consolation by them. The more carefully we listen, the clearer His voice becomes. We can pray through our day-to-day situations. When we do so, we will effectively be able to communicate our faith in Him to others.

Chapter 20

The Rewards of Hope

Are you wallowing in the pit of despair? Has pessimism put you there? If so, Satan is applauding and cheering because he has you where he wants you. In every situation, we can choose to be either negative or positive. Being negative causes pessimism, but being positive brings hope. When we're hopeful, our hearts soar through the air like kites.

When we told my grandfather that my grandmother died two days earlier, he was distraught and gave up hope. He went to bed that evening and never woke up—it was as if he had given up all hope. Even the medical field now recognizes the power of hope.

Doctors sometimes reschedule surgery if a patient is feeling discouraged and down. But hope gives birth to renewed courage and strength. Hope greatly affects our physical, mental, and spiritual well being.

Prayer also strengthens hope. When we pray, we admit that we're unable to control our own circumstances. We turn them over to God, and then wait expectantly for His intervention in our lives. God's love and understanding liberate us from our fears providing us with immeasurable possibilities. Once we do everything we can to help our situation, the results are in God's hands. We can rest assured that the outcome will be in our best interest.

Dressed in encouragement, we become positively infectious. Kids would realize that every time they hope to sink a basketball, they'd be praying for God's intervention. Transformed with energy, we're restored with a drive that enables us to exhaust ourselves for God. In the same way, hope gives us zeal for life. Trusting in God replenishes us to go another mile, even if we don't know how.

Philippians 4:13 tells us:

> "I can do everything through Him who gives me strength."

When we truly believe this, we're placing our destiny in the hands of God. He becomes the pilot and we His passengers. Relinquishing control to God and walking in obedience permits us to eagerly begin our day with the hope that all will work out in accordance with His plan for our lives. We can be confident that He's always with us, helping us carry our cross.

Since our behavior follows our thought process, thinking negatively binds us with chains and brings us down. By thinking positively, we shed this feeling of hopelessness; and in turn, we will act constructively. Relying on God like children and believing in His promises, we empower ourselves to make better choices that are more conducive to honoring Him. This, in turn, propels us to greater heights.

In reading Ephesians 6:12–13, we're reminded that the struggle to overcome cynicism is not with the person we are confronting or ourselves for that matter, but with the spiritual forces of evil. Therefore, we must love the sinner and hate the sin:

> "For our struggle is not against flesh and blood, but against the rulers, against the authorities, against the powers of this dark world and against the spiritual forces of evil in the heavenly realms. Therefore, put on the full armor of God, so that when the day of evil comes, you may be able to stand your ground, and after you have done everything, to stand."

Discovering hope is as simple as reaching out to God and casting our cares upon Him. It resides within us waiting to escalate our hearts to a higher place. When we need hope, it's immediately available to us. In choosing to become victims of darkness, we're like children of a king sitting hopelessly in rags outside an open gate to a castle where a treasure of riches lies waiting for us to receive.

God manifests Himself to us in so many ways—through the laughter of a child, the warmth of a sunset, the softness of music, or the sweetness and harmony of nature. His artwork is everywhere surrounding us with His presence. His omniscient wisdom dictates our lives like a rudder steers a ship.

By resisting pessimism, we consciously choose to bask in God's splendor and find our strength in Him. The rewards of hope are infinite.

Chapter 21
The Art of Compassion

"Congratulations, you're pregnant."

The doctor's words came so nonchalantly. I'm forty-three years old and have raised three children, who are now ages 17, 18, and 19. When I went home to tell Charlie the wonderful news, somehow he seemed more shocked than delighted. I thought we shared the same concerns.

"Well, if God thinks we can do it, then we can do it. I know, with His help, we can do anything." I tried to convince him.

We didn't tell anyone because I wasn't up to answering silly questions like: "Were you planning this?" Or, "Do you really want to go through raising children again when yours are already grown?" I knew someone would make a remark about the odds for having a healthy baby after the age of forty. Oh, I knew God would give me the words to say to them:

> "But when they arrest you, do not worry about what to say or how to say it. At that time you will be given what to say, for it will not be you speaking, but the Spirit of your Father speaking through you."
>
> Mt 10:19

Of course, we quietly canceled our summer trip to Europe with our family. We'd find a way to break the news to them sooner or later. Oh, there would have to be some adjustments. But we had no trouble clearing the calendar and making the necessary changes. This was a wonderful blessing.

Each time I went to the doctor's office, I was greeted with the warmest compassion. In spite of my insecurities for raising a baby again at my age, the staff was very encouraging and answered all of my naïve questions. I felt like a dinosaur, since the latest technology flooded the market. I'd have to read up on all the new techniques for child rearing. How much could things have changed?

As the doctor stared at the sonogram screen, I thought it looked somewhat like a television on which you couldn't quite adjust the picture. He asked me to look at the screen so I could see the pregnancy sac. He seemed concerned because he couldn't find the heartbeat of the fetus. I admitted that the dates I gave him of my last menstrual cycle might have been wrong.

"The baby is so small, how could you ever expect to find a heartbeat so young?" I asked. That pretty much exemplified the capacity of my knowledge of modern technology.

"Come back next week, and we'll try again." He stated, concerned.

I agreed, and tried to maintain a stable composure. Satan knows when to intrude, and he certainly thrives on doubt. I knew I shouldn't let my thoughts run away in a negative direction. I prayed unceasingly. *God, please let this baby have a chance to live.* I never experienced the loss of a baby before. All of my pregnancies were normal and healthy. How could anything be wrong?

When I went back to the doctor's office, his first words to me were:

"If I can't find a heartbeat today, I'll really be concerned."

After reviewing the snowy screen of the sonogram, he confirmed that there was no viable fetus inside my womb.

When I left the office, it seemed like all eyes were on me. How did everyone know what the outcome of this visit was? All I did was get dressed, collect my things, and open the door. The staff looked at me with such compassion, which I thought was non-existent in today's sterile, secular world. They seemed to feel my pain and understand my loss.

"Are you going to be all right?" they inquired.

"Sure," I responded, not quite grasping the reality of it all.

They seemed to know what emotions lie in wait ahead of me and were ready to become a blanket of empathy. *This is what's missing in the world,* I thought, *the art of compassion.* I'm grateful for friends who know how to paint a picture of compassion in the hearts of those who are hurting. I pray that I will be able to emulate such warmth and kindness to those in need of God's love.

In this hustled and harried world we live in, and given the fast pace of our schedules, we have left little room for compassion. I found it that day in the hearts of my doctor, his staff, and good, spiritual friends. I want to be able to offer compassion to all the hurting people out there that don't even have to express their thoughts. I want to react warmly to them, as these wonderful people reacted to me; feeling my pain by reaching out with their eyes and hearts.

We never know how others might be suffering on the inside. Not everyone shares his or her pain. Let's offer them our empathy. Whenever we encounter another person, we have the opportunity to show God's love. It's His spirit that lives in each and every one of us. Would we do any less for Jesus? Our anger would be defused, our hearts would ignite, and we would be exercising the unconditional love God meant for us to share.

Chapter 22
Hang On and Enjoy the Ride!

How many times have you sat around and mulled over situations you have no idea how to face? I know I've been the world's greatest procrastinator when it comes to confronting issues. Usually, I just plug along and hope that things will work themselves out. Well, not anymore. I strive to see problems as opportunities for growth.

God has proven to me over and over again that He's much better at handling those tough situations than I am. My job is to trust Him then hang on and enjoy the ride. I once read a sign that said, "If you are in the driver's seat, and God is your co-pilot, switch seats." What a wonderful idea.

He knows what He needs us to do. He designed each one of us for a specific purpose. Our gifts have been given to us so that we may share them with others. They're like money in the bank that grows with interest. Our talents and skills only improve when we use them for the good of others. There's no greater joy than giving. We receive so much more gratification when we share our blessings.

Think of all the great artists, musicians, preachers, and teachers in the world. How sad it would be if they never shared their talent with the rest of the world. We would be lacking the great inspiration they instill within us to try our hand at something.

You'd be surprised at the amount of budding artists who would soar if their endeavors were fueled with encouragement. We need to share kind comments that build up rather than tear down. The effects are so abundant

When I went back to college, I was procrastinating because I was petrified of taking the entrance exam (which is really only a placement test). I would constantly tell myself that I couldn't do the math. Yet I had this unquenchable desire to learn. My work has been becoming more and more voluminous, and I've been feeling stagnant. I find it funny how God designed us to need one another. I had to ask Nancy to help me.

One day, as she was explaining yet another algebra problem, she said, "Mommy, you look like you're about to cry." Well, I did. I cried and I cried until finally, I stopped feeling sorry for myself and left the pity party once and for all.

On the day I was scheduled to take the test, I prayed, "God, I know You are with me and will help me overcome my fears. I trust You, and I'll do my best—let's just do it!"

I walked through the bustling campus feeling rejuvenated. I breathed in the fresh, crisp air and felt a renewed peace and strength wash over me. Like all tasks that seem insurmountable, we need to break them down into smaller parts. Hence, God designed the days of the week. Remember the Our Father: "**Give us this day, our daily bread.**" Each day has enough of its own difficulties—there's no need to add on tomorrow's.

When I sat for the exam, I was so happy to answer the preliminary questions. How long has it been since you've taken algebra? How many years has it been since you have taken English in high school? Is English your primary language? This made me realize that there were others who felt the same anxiety that I did. There were immigrants in this country that had a greater handicap than I did taking this test, wanting to learn more; and they were doing it. *O.K., God, we can do this together!* I convinced myself.

I gave careful thought to each question. Thank God the test was not timed. I think I could have spent three meal periods there. I was given one piece of scrap paper, since calculators were not permitted; but, of course, I requested one fourth of the stack. As I was knocking off each question, which I was pleased to discover was multiple choice (another blessing), I felt an enormous burden lift from my shoulders. God helped me overcome my fear, sit down, and take the test. This was a tremendous accomplishment for me. That in itself was so gratifying.

On another occasion, Anthony and I were taking our two dogs to an owner training class. I say owner training because the dogs are fine, it's the owners that need the training. The trainer made a comment to me that reduced me to tears. He said:

"Lady, some day this dog is going to bite you or somebody else."

I wanted to say to him,

"Why do you think I'm here?"

But I didn't. I just cried. On the drive home, I spent a good amount of time sulking. I complained to Anthony that I didn't want to go back there and was going to quit the class. He said to me:

"Mommy, would you please stop feeling sorry for yourself and quit bawling?"

It was then that I realized that I was not being a very good role model for him. He was showing me how to hang in there and face the music. I now know why the children were so important to Jesus. It's their trusting faith, their ability to be resilient, courageous, curious, and zealous. They don't know how they are going to accomplish anything. They don't consider the means or the consequences; they just do it.

I hope that we can trust in God that our lives have been predestined by Him. He has created each one of us for a unique purpose with specific gifts to build up His kingdom. Think of all the talents we are complimented for and love doing. Activities that we just seem to flourish in and thrive on are special abilities that God has knitted within us in order for us to contribute to the fabric of His people.

In everything we do, let's offer it up as a sacrifice to our loving God for all the magnificent blessings He has given to us. We are a remarkable group of people who can choose to trust in His omnipotence. Let's celebrate our differences, live well, love much, and laugh often.

Coming Soon:

Live Well, Love Much, Laugh Often Audio Series Tapes & CDs
Live Well, Love Much, Laugh Often Workbook
Live Well, Love Much, Laugh Often Devotional Journal
Live Well, Love Much, Laugh Often Reusable Devotional Calendar
Live Well, Love Much, Laugh Often on Charity
Live Well, Love Much, Laugh Often on Gratitude
Live Well, Love Much, Laugh Often on Courage
Live Well, Love Much, Laugh Often on Forgiveness
Live Well, Love Much, Laugh Often on Trust
Live Well, Love Much, Laugh Often on Patience
Live Well, Love Much, Laugh Often on Self Control
Live Well, Love Much, Laugh Often on Grace
Live Well, Love Much, Laugh Often on Perseverance

www.ingramcontent.com/pod-product-compliance
Lightning Source LLC
Chambersburg PA
CBHW052057070526
44584CB00017B/2216